Images of Nottingham

Images of Nottingham

The
Breedon Books
Publishing Company
Derby

Published in Great Britain by
The Breedon Books Publishing Company Limited
Breedon House, 44 Friar Gate, Derby, DE1 1DA
1994

ISBN 1 873626 83 5

Printed and bound by Butler and Tanner Limited, Frome and London.
Jackets printed by BDC Printing Services Limited of Derby

Contents

Foreword
by Sue Pollard

THERE are many great places to come from – I can think of dozens I would rather come from than go to.

But Nottingham is not one of them. I'm Nottingham born and bred and proud of it – I love the city, the people . . .everything about it, so *Images of Nottingham* brings back some wonderful memories, honest mi duck!

I was teased over my glasses at Peveril School in Aspley, developing a comedy routine to combat it, had my first serious kiss in the Castle grounds, tripped the light fantastic at the Palais – usually on to my face – and learned my trade in local amateur dramatics.

I could say I loved my job at the Tennant Rubber Company in Carlton Road, but that would be stretching it too far!

Queen of the Midlands? I met him once in Clumber Street, I think.

Seriously, though, Nottingham is a great place and I love going back home. See you there soon.

Introduction

NOTTINGHAM has turned steadily but surely towards full circle since 1796 when gentlewoman and diarist Celia Fiennes admiringly observed a 'very fine prospect' from the sandstone cliff of Castle Rock.

By the 1840s, the 'beautiful and pleasant' elegance described by novelist Daniel Defoe (1660-1731) when the population numbered barely 10,000 had been badly scarred with more than 50,000 people living in the largely squalid confines of the medieval town.

This deteriorated further into a maze of 'mean streets, alleyways, courts, filth and misery beyond belief' after the Nottingham Enclosure Act of 1845 was at least partly responsible for a population invasion which turned it into one of the most overcrowded towns in England, leading to a mean age of death of little more than 11 years in one sub-district of St Ann's.

Seventy years ago, the view from the rock was still blighted by a hotchpotch of ugliness. But much of this has gone and not for nothing was Nottinghamshire, with Nottingham itself making a telling contribution, voted Holiday Destination of the Year by the English Tourist Board in November, 1993.

The renaissance of Nottingham as a great place in which to live has been achieved by largely judicious clearance, preservation and development. It is a tribute to successive councils, businesses and, most of all, to its people.

They go back a long time. Nottingham became a city in 1897 but the original settlement of Snotingaham was set up in about 500AD on land lived on, now and again, from the later Stone Age. The pages of the town's history are mainly blank for the first three centuries but it is recorded that in 868, the Vikings came 'with dreadfulness', although they agreed to retire without a battleaxe raised after the King of Mercia sent in the forces of his brothers-in-law Ethelred, King of Wessex, and Alfred, only to return later, leading eventually to the town becoming one of their five royal boroughs, fortified centres of the Danelaw.

Stately St Mary's Church, one of the finest town churches in England, occupies a central position in the ancient 'English' borough, which also houses the old commercial and professional centre among the tangle of streets in the Lace Market; while the old 'French' borough, which was a Norman settlement

The prospect of Nottingham when it was an enclosed town in 1677, from Derby Road on the west side.

The South View of Nottingham, a copper engraving of 1790.

Another southerly view of Nottingham from a print published in 1808.

Nottingham from the Park Side, a painting by M.Webster in about 1840.

A prospect of County Hall as it was in 1730.

protected by the walls of Nottingham Castle, contains the Playhouse, the Royal Centre and the cinemas. Old Market Square, the biggest market place in England, started off as a no man's land between the two boroughs but was later embraced within the 80 acres of the Norman borough, although by the twelfth century it was used by both communities.

Nottingham Castle

Top: An old engraving of Nottingham Castle when it belonged to the Duke of Newcastle. The original fortress was built by order of William the Conqueror in 1068. It was improved during the reign of successive kings and reached its pinnacle in the days of Edward IV (1461-1483). It was often used by reigning monarchs, but by Henry VII's reign it was in ruins. The Earl of Rutland took it off the hands of James I, demolished parts of it and sold some of the stones, so that by 1692, only the walls remained.

Middle: The burning of the 1679 version of Nottingham Castle by Reform Bill Rioters in October 1831 from T.Allom's drawing of 1840. By the end of the nineteenth century, part of the castle was let to tenants, part housed a school for young ladies and another section was an armoury. The end of the Civil War had heralded the close of the original castle's long history as a military stronghold and an order for its demolition was obtained in 1651. The shell was returned to the Earl of Rutland's estate and it was sold to the Duke of Newcastle in 1674. He started a new castle building and his son completed it three years after the duke's death in 1676.

Right: A reward poster offering £500 and a pardon for anyone offering information about the rioters who burned down Nottingham Castle.

The Nottingham Castle gateway before its restoration in 1900.

A memorial in Nottingham Castle grounds to officers and men of the 59th Regiment (Old 2nd Notts) Regiment of Foot, pictured in 1917.

An aerial view of Nottingham Castle and grounds in 1937. The baroque mansion of the late seventeenth century was restored in the nineteenth century as the first municipal museum of England.

Nottingham Castle entrance as it looked in July 1942, before part of it was demolished.

A workman cuts away loose sandstone from Castle Rock after a fall of stone in September 1937.

A view of Nottingham Castle in 1957.

Cables are laid in 1946 to convert Nottingham Castle from gaslight to electricity.

A view from Nottingham Castle grounds in about 1948.

Nottingham Castle gate as it was in 1950.

The sundial illustrated was erected to the memory of the 17th Battalion (Welbeck Rangers) Sherwood Foresters, who lost their lives in the Great War of 1914-18. It stands in the castle's grounds

Old Market Square

Nottingham's Old Market Square is nearly three-quarters of a mile in circumference and is the biggest in England. Slabs replaced the colourful stalls when the open market moved to a covered area in Huntingdon Street in the 1920s, leading to the nickname 'Slab Square'. The Goose Fair moved from the square to The Forest after the 1927 event.

What a turnout. This undated picture was taken in Nottingham Great Market Place, now Old Market Square.

The last night of the fish and chip stalls in Nottingham's Great Market Place in October 1928.

The opening of Nottingham's new Council House in 1929. The ceremony was carried out by the Prince of Wales on 22 May. The architect was Nottingham-born T.Cecil Howett and the great clock there was named Little John.

The Arcade in the Council House in the 1920s.

Trent Bridge

Trent Bridge spans more than 1,000 years. The first one was built in about 922, with major restoration work in 1158. In 1457 the badly neglected bridge collapsed. It was repaired but the great flood of 1683 swept it away. The bridge was rebuilt but there was more severe flood damage in 1726 and by the middle of the nineteenth century, it was in a dangerous state. A newly-built bridge was completed in 1871 and in 1926 its width was doubled to 80 feet.

One of the old arches at Trent Bridge.

Trent Bridge, possibly in the 1920s after a widening scheme had been completed.

Trent Bridge with the Town Arms in the distance. The picture is believed to have been taken in 1935.

Busy, but not that busy by today's standards. Traffic at Trent Bridge in 1936.

The Goose Fair

This little chap is obviously quite happy to grasp the long arm of the law after getting lost at the 1955 Goose Fair.

There was already an eight-day Nottingham Goose Fair in 1284 and the event is world renowned, as one of t

...dest, biggest and best. Traffic problems forced it out from Old Market Square to The Forest after 1927.

Glorious sunshine for the 1946 Goose Fair.

Times change but Goose Fair magic goes on for ever and the delight on these young faces in 1970 shows why.

Tillie, a pet goose owned by Mrs Sari Brinn, decides to take a look around the Forest Recreation Ground at the 607th Goose Fair in 1965.

The bells, the bells. Goose Fair 1975 is opened by Council Mrs Ivy Matthews, Nottingham's first woman Lord Mayor.

All the fun of the fair as the Lord Mayor and Lady Mayoress of Nottingham, Alderman and Mrs Charles Butler, try a ride on one of the Goose Fair roundabouts in 1972.

A packed house at Nottingham Goose Fair in 1978.

Nottingham's Caves

Nottingham is honeycombed by hundreds of caves, the most famous being Mortimer's Hole from where, in 1330, a group of conspirators were said to have entered Nottingham Castle to capture Roger, Earl of Mortimer, lover of Queen Isabella, widow of the murdered Edward III. Mortimer was later executed at Tyburn. Deep beneath the Broad Marsh shopping centre is a labyrinth of caves dating back at least 700 years. The caves, which are quite warm and dry, have been used by religious minorities, leather tanners and publicans over the centuries and some of them became air-raid shelters during the last war.

Mr D. White, the contractor's site agent, climbs down, in 1974, a 20ft shaft which leads to a cave once used as a cellar by the Eight Bells public house.

An old, undated picture of the entrance to the Ropewalk caves in Nottingham.

A party of tourists looks over the Drury Hill caves in March 1978.

The Rock Cemetery caves in Nottingham.

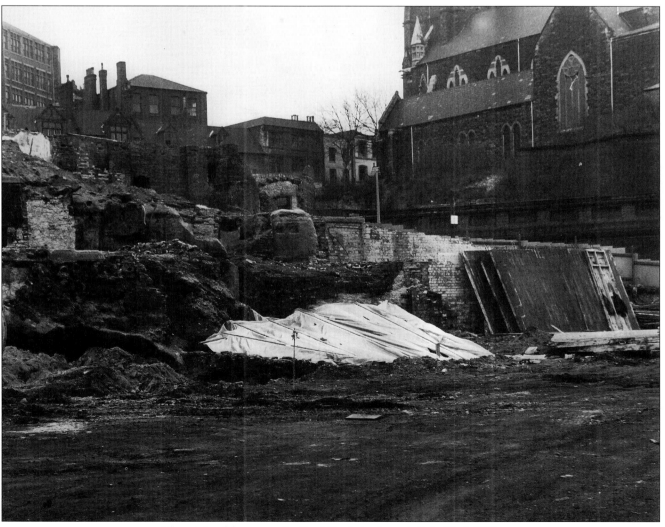

The exterior of the caves on the Broad Marsh development site in March 1971.

The layout of the lesser-known caves on Mansfield Road, Nottingham.

This carving of Daniel in the Lions' Den was rediscovered in 1988, in a cave under Nottingham, after lying hidden for many years. The biblical scene was created in Victorian times for an alderman's garden but never saw the light of day. Researchers Jenny Owen and Jenny Walsby found the carving of a 121ft lion, a lioness and Daniel minus his arms on a bed of pebbly sandstone in the Nottingham Castle formation that year while compiling a register and map for the British Geological Survey at Keyworth, but this picture was taken in July 1942.

Mr A.G.MacCormick, keeper of antiquities at Nottingham Museum in 1974, emerges from one of the shallower caves which had been found on the Farmer's Yard site in Nottingham.

One of the passages in the Guildhall site caves, which are 30ft below the surface and are believed to be of Saxon origin.

The stairway beside a well in the caves underneath Houndsgate, pictured in November 1956.

A cave under Ye Olde Salutation Inn.

The entrance to the underground well and storage tank, known as the Admiral's Bath, at the bottom of these steps at Wollaton Hall. The water to these wells is so clear that the bottom is clearly visible, even at a depth at eight or nine feet.

Cave houses in Sneinton – an undated picture.

City Centre and Suburbs

The Robin Hood statue below the Castle. There is surprisingly little in Nottingham's history to connect Robin Hood with the city, but Robin appears in literature from the early fifteenth century. He is said to have married Maid Marian in Edwinstowe Church and to have died on 18 November 1247.

They never said Robin
Hood was this tall.
The toddler marvelling
at the giant statue in
Market Street which
formed part of
Nottingham's
Christmas decorations
in 1982 is Danielle
Roche of Bingham.

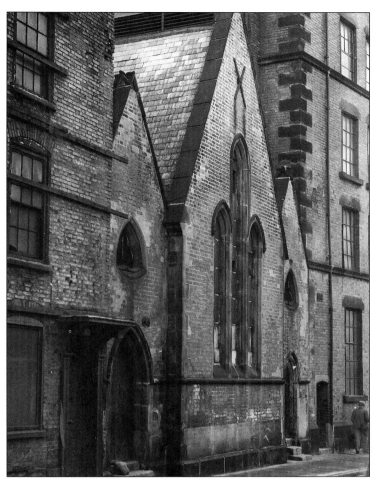

Left and above: The dungeons at Nottingham's Shire Hall court and jail, a place of hangings and judicial cruelty for hundreds of years. The ball and chains stripped the flesh from the legs.

The Shire Hall, High Pavement, Nottingham. It was redesigned and rebuilt in about 1768-1770 but in 1876, T.C.Hine tore down the building, leaving only the façade.

Once described as a 'typical example of a medieval street', Drury Hill, Nottingham's oldest thoroughfare, at one time carried most of the traffic from the centre of the old Saxon borough to the south, across The Meadows and, in later days, to Sussex Street, the Midland Station and Trent Bridge. It was once called Vault Lane and it crossed the course of the River Leen.

Left: An undated picture of Bridlesmith Gate.

The Old Town Hall, Weekday Cross, where once the Assizes were held. The picture is dated 1937.

King John's Chambers thoroughfare connecting Bridlesmith Gate and Fletcher Gate. The view is looking towards the former.

The slum, pictured in the 1930s, on which Nottingham's new wholesale market was built at the Sneinton end of Carlton Road.

Hounds Gate, looking towards St Peter's Church, in 1946. Before the medieval castle obstructed it, Hounds Gate was the city's primary road to the west.

Hounds Gate from the Castle end on 2 September 1947, the day it became a one-way street.

Alderman James Huthwaite's house, built in 1740, on Spaniel Row, Nottingham.

This building in Spaniel Row, Nottingham, was erected as a Friend's Meeting House and was converted into a Catholic Apostolic Church in 1850. Later, it was used as a bleach house.

The site of the erection of King Charles I's standard in Standard Hill.

The post office in Queen Street as it was in March 1938.

Queen Street from the Council House. This picture was taken around 1931 but the view is still recognisable today.

Left: The Borough Club, which opened in the 1890s. It was non-political. Right: Tennants Nottingham Brewery, Mansfield Road, pictured in 1953.

The Exchange area of Nottingham as it was in 1926.

The scene in Colwick Road in May, 1965.

Long Row and the Council House in the centre of Nottingham.

Theatre Square and Parliament Street in the 1920s.

An undated picture of Parker's shop in Union Road, Nottingham. Note the offer on the wall 'Boots all shapes' — they were priced at 10s 6d.

World War One guns at Wollaton Park for a Gun Week, date unknown.

Another historic address in Nottingham which was demolished soon after this picture was taken in 1964. It was the house in Birkland Avenue at which James Barrie lodged when he worked for the Nottingham Journal. That was in 1883-84 before Barrie became famous for Peter Pan and a long list of other books and plays. It was one of a number of buildings that had to go to make way for a new Civic Centre.

An inscription on a wall outside the Shire Hall telling the tale of a man hanged for 'house braking'.

Above and below: The exterior of Dakeyne Street Lad's Club in 1934 – and the reading room.

Above and right: Mount Square before major re-development work was undertaken.

Gordon Road, formerly Long Hedge Lane, as it was in May 1965.

Star Court thoroughfare yard, Mount Street, early this century.

Sunshine and shadow in St James's Street, Nottingham, in February 1956.

Lower Parliament Street, Nottingham, year unknown.

Charlotte Street before the turn of the century. The building in the centre of the road is a public urinal.

Another picture of Charlotte Street taken around 1895.

The bustling Sneinton market in July 1963 and a spot of music at The Market. Year not known.

An old print of Nottingham's Arboretum.

Nottingham Arboretum Rooms in 1932. The wings were declared unsafe at about the time this picture was taken and were demolished, leaving only the centre blocks of the building.

Autumn shadows lengthen as schoolgirls make their way home through Nottingham Arboretum in September, 1960.

A Nottingham Arboretum Crimea War memorial, with the Chinese Bell, taken by Nottinghamshire soldiers from 'a large and handsome temple near the East Gate of Canton'. The memorial is dedicated to local men who fell in 1845-55 during the war. The cannons were brought over from it by a local regiment. The Chinese Bell from the Crimea War memorial in Nottingham soon after it had been removed because it was considered unsafe in 1955.

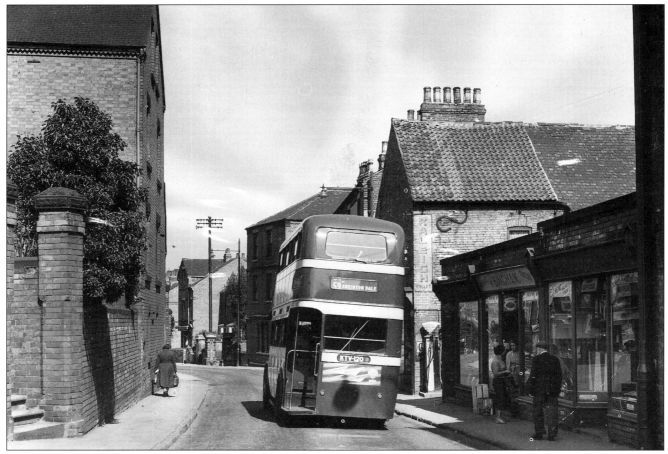

One of the narrow spots on Sneinton Dale in 1955.

Queen's Walk in 1903.

The police station at the corner of Queen's Walk and Kirkwhite Street East, looking up Queen's River towards the LMS Station in 1936.

The scene at Canning Circus, at the junction of Derby Road and Alfreton Road in 1938, with Boots the Chemists, centre.

An aerial view of Nottingham's city centre with the Castle in the foreground.

Robin Hood Terrace, leading into Victoria Park, in 1936.

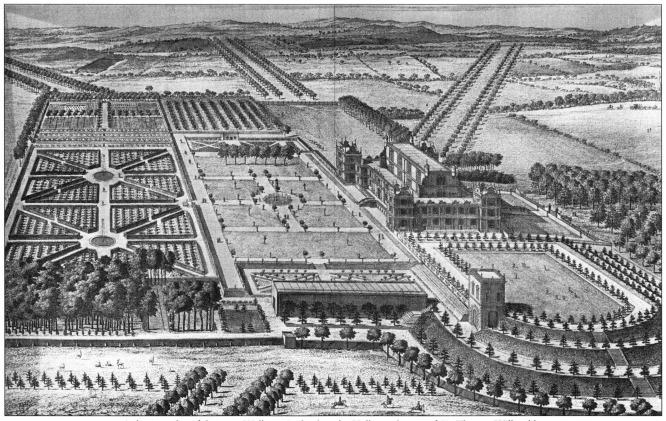

A classic garden of the past, Wollaton Park when the Hall was the seat of Sir Thomas Willoughby.

The new, in 1963, Bath Street Police Station, commended by the Civic Trust Award scheme.

Taken just before its demolition, the old Bath Street Police Station.

Garner's Hill, Nottingham, in 1921.

The Jews Cemetery in Nottingham. The picture is believed to have been taken in 1931.

A fine example of back-to-back houses in St Ann's in 1952.

Trinity Square, with the remains of Holy Trinity Church, in July 1958. The site is now occupied by a multi-storey car-park.

A bird's eye view of Trinity Square in February 1960.

The Park – Village Within a City

The Park, a 155-acre private housing estate in the centre of Nottingham, was planned by the Fifth Duke of Newcastle in 1851 as a peaceful haven for lace barons and other entrepreneurs. There are more than 650 homes, of all shapes and sizes, mostly built between 1854 and 1887, with circuses, drives and crescents, some tree-lined. The Park is still cut off by gates but a large tunnel to it under The Ropewalk was boarded up in 1962.

The Park steps in April 1946.

The tunnel from The Park end.

A view of Peveril Drive, The Park, in the 1930s.

Great Men of Nottinghamshire

Bendigo, real name William Abendigo Thomson, who was born in Parliament Street, Nottingham, was champion bare-knuckle prizefighter of England although he weighed only 12 stones. In 18 years he lost only one fight, a dubious decision to Ben Caunt, which he later avenged. The referee gave Caunt the verdict in the 73rd round when Bendigo, wearing ordinary boots, slipped and fell on the turf. But in the return, in September 1845, Bendigo, giving away three stones in weight, won in the 93rd round when Caunt fell exhausted. Bendigo was jailed 28 times after he retired undefeated but later beat his drink problem and became a well-known local preacher. He died in 1880, aged 69.

Emile Degand, the Belgian flyweight champion, visits Bendigo's grave in Bath Street cemetery, Nottingham, in January 1953. Degand was in the city for a fight with George Marsden, which he lost.

The Rest Garden in Bath Street, where Bendigo was laid to rest. The original caption in May, 1953, says: 'Holy Trinity's spire has gone and St Matthew's soon will.' The place was turned from the dread burial ground for cholera victims into a pleasant mini-park. Bendigo did not die of cholera but as the result of a fall.

The daring deeds of World War One flying ace Albert Ball have always been the stuff of legends. He shot down 30 enemy aeroplanes and was nicknamed the 'English Richthofen' by the Germans after their own hero the Red Baron. Ball was undoubtedly one of the greatest pilots of his time but he was killed in a dogfight on 17 May 1917 when he was only 20 years old. A month later he was awarded the Victoria Cross 'for the most conspicuous and consistent bravery'. Ball grew up in Lenton and The Park, Nottingham.

A Colt automatic pistol carried by Captain Albert Ball, VC, during World War One. It is one of a collection of Ball's relics in the Castle Museum.

The barony of the estate of Newstead, Nottinghamshire, passed to Lord Byron (George Gordon, the poet , 1788-1824) when he was ten years old. He wrote his first poems while a schoolboy at Harrow and a small volume of verse, Fugitive Pieces, was published in 1807 while he was at Cambridge University. His satire, English Bards and Scotch Reviewers, made him famous and he never looked back.

Above: William Booth, who was born in 1829 in Sneinton, Nottingham, became founder and first general of the Salvation Army in 1877 and remained in office until his death in 1912.

The novelist D.H.Lawrence (1885-1930), a miner's son born at Eastwood, Nottinghamshire, won a £12-a-year county scholarship to Nottingham High School when he was 12. When he left school in 1901, he worked as a junior clerk in the city, becoming seriously ill with pneumonia when he was 16. Later, he went to Nottingham University College and became a teacher like his mother. His first novel The White Peacock *was published in 1911 and he gave up teaching for writing.* Sons and Lovers, *for many the favourite of Lawrence's novels, was published in 1913. His publishers were prosecuted for alleged obscenity when* The Rainbow *came out and all copies were confiscated.* Lady Chatterley's Lover *was started after Lawrence left England for Italy in 1926 and was first published in 1928 but not in England in its unexpurgated form until 1961, after a trial in which the English literary establishment closed ranks against the censor.*

Transport in Nottingham

Excavation work being carried out at the Victoria Station site in around 1890. Some of those who worked on it were quite young. Boys were often employed as tip drivers and to keep the wagon wheels greased.

The Victoria Station was constructed between 1890 and 1900 and this is one of many gangs of navvies working on the line. They earned about 20 shillings (£1) a week.

Excavation for the Victoria Station, looking north. The footbridge was on a site at Charlotte Street.

All ready to go. Nottingham Victoria Station in 1900, soon after it opened for business.

The last passenger train pulls out of Nottingham Victoria Station in September 1967, a sad day for its driver George Chambers, who remembered the old bustling station.

The J11 class 0-6-0 locomotive of the former Great Central Railway ready for a last run special.

The Master Cutler in Victoria Station in 1952. The last steam train left there in September 1966.

The doors close for the final time at Victoria Station.

Chief Inspector J.Mason at one of the controls of the new ticket machines on Nottingham City Transport's newly-introduced one-man buses in July 1971.

Off on holiday. The scene at the Victoria Station in August 1950.

A Pioneer bus belonging to the Mansfield Motor Car Co, which was formed in April 1898. It had a seating capacity of 22 passengers with provision for a trailer to carry 22 more.

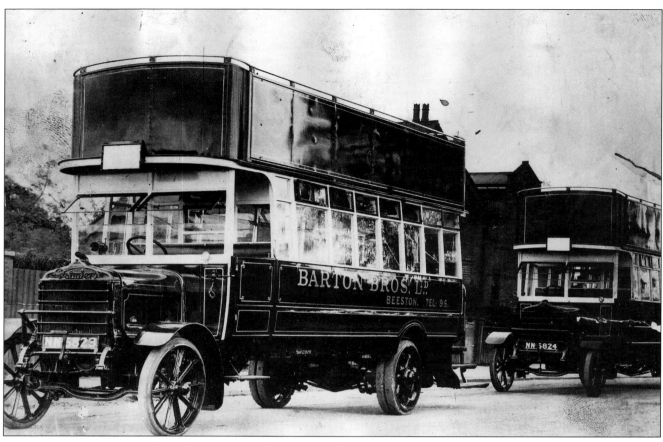

A Barton Bros Y-type Daimler 64-seater double decker pictured in Nottingham in 1920.

A Robin Hood Coaches vehicle en route in Nottingham in 1950.

An undated picture of trams in service on Woodborough Road, Nottingham.

This picture is not as old as it might seem. George Hopkins was the conductor of the horse-drawn bus, operating between Walter Fountain and Abbey Bridge, Lenton, as part of the City Transport Department's Golden Jubilee celebrations in 1947.

Above and below: Horse-drawn tramcars of the types used 50 years before, on exhibition in 1947, at the Nottingham Corporation Transport Department maintenance department at Trent Bridge, as part of the Golden Jubilee celebrations.

A 1938 picture of a horse-bus in Market Place, Bulwell.

Nottingham Corporation's oldest trolleybus, still in service when this picture was taken in 1948.

A new 'trackless bus' pictured in June, 1929.

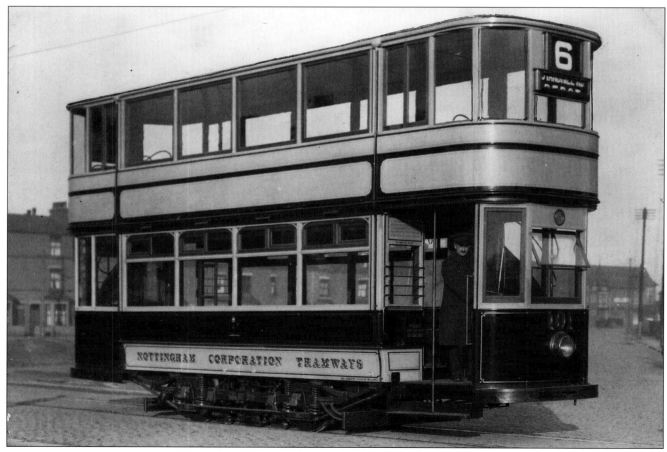

This was described as a new type of Nottingham tramcar in January, 1927.

Just the job for a tough winter – a Nottingham Tramways snow plough.

A 'bus jam' in Nottingham in January 1965, caused when the trolley wires failed. 'It happens all too often these days', said the original caption.

A once familiar sight on the Nottingham-Long Eaton road, A replica of Barton's 1908 charabanc, pictured on a trial run in June 1953.

Tram number 57 on Mansfield Road, Nottingham in the 1920s.

A pair of narrow boats working the Nottingham Canal. Year unknown.

Carrington LNER station in April 1930. It closed two years earlier.

Nottingham's first railway station, the Midland, in about 1840.

The Lord Mayor of Nottingham unveiling the nameplate on the new Robin Hood Nottingham-London express at the Midland Station in February 1959.

The clock is turned back more than 20 years as the steam era returns to the Midland Station in June 1987 in the form of a Class Seven freight locomotive.

Heavy traffic on the River Trent at Trent Bridge, year unknown.

Rail enthusiasts boarding the last diesel from Nottingham Arkwright Street to Rugby – when the train had gone the station closed for the last time. The passenger service through there was withdrawn in May 1969.

The busy Nottingham Canal between Wilford Road and Carrington Street in the late 1920s.

Nottingham at War

Lady Reading, centre, chairman of the WVS, inspects the Queen's Messengers Convoy personnel in Nottingham after their return from service in Liverpool.

Nottingham members of the LNER decontamination and carriage cleaners.

A wartime ice-cream seller serves three attractive customers in Nottingham.

University College in Shakespeare Street after the Nottingham blitz.

Wholesale destruction in Shakespeare Street after the blitz.

The gutted mining department at University College.

All that remains of 27 to 47 Hutton Street, Trent Lane, Nottingham after a raid by German bombers in January, 1941.

A bomb crater at Trent Bridge cricket ground.

The Boots gymnasium block after the raid.

Left: More severe bomb damage at the Boots Publicity warehouse site. Right: The old bottle washing department at Boots.

The remains of a draper's shop in Nottingham.

All that was left of the Trivett's building in Short Hill, Nottingham, after the raid.

Victory celebrations. The scene in Old Market Square on VE Day, 8 May 1945, as Winston Churchill was broadcasting to the nation.

Victory celebrations in the city centre.

A Nottingham soldier gets a special thank you as Nottingham celebrates victory.

Two street parties in Nottingham as part of victory celebrations.

Nottingham's first woman taxi driver all ready to go in March 1916, during World War One.

Women electricians at Nottingham Victoria Station in 1917.

Health and Learning

The Tuberculosis Clinic in Gregory Boulevard, Nottingham, in 1929.

Nottingham's Queen's Medical Centre picture in 1981. It cost more than £70 million and opened as a teaching hospital integrated with Nottingham University. The first in-patients were admitted in December 1978. They were all children. The transfer followed the closure of the Children's Hospital in Berkeley Avenue in November that year.

Nottingham University in its picturesque setting on University Boulevard.

Pupils of Brincliffe Grammar School, Nottingham, on course for a lesson in 1957.

An old picture of Nottingham College of Art and Technology in Waverley Street.

*Brincliffe County
Grammar School for
Girls in 1950.*

Nottingham High School for Boys at St Mary's Church on Founder's Day in 1929.

Storytime . . .and Mrs O.Browne, leader of the Good Shepherd pre-school playgroup at Woodthorpe prepares to weave a magic spell of words over her lively charges at the first session of the term in September 1968.

Some of the 180 children from Clifton Estate, who started their term in 1954 at Clifton Hall, which had been owned by the Clifton family for 900 years. A Clifton received the land from William the Conqueror soon after the Battle of Hastings in 1066. The teacher pointing out some of the features of the stately mansion is Mrs K.Spiers.

The class of 1925 at Bluecoat School, Mansfield Road, Nottingham. Bluecoat was founded as a charity school in 1706 on Weekday Cross, moved to Mansfield Road and was later relocated on Aspley Lane.

An aerial picture of Nottingham General Hospital taken by the RAF in 1950. The General was funded by public subscription and opened in 1782 for the 'relief of poor persons'.

The Women's Hospital, Peel Street in 1981. A women's hospital was instituted in Castle Gate in 1875.

An outdoor sketching lesson for pupils of Trent Bridge Junior School near the Suspension Bridge in June 1961.

The Broadgate School, in The Park, in 1971.

The old St Ann's School which was later taken over by the Nottingham Auxiliary Fire Service.

Miss Ada Gillett's Standard IV music class at Mapperley's Walter Halls Primary School, in Querneby Road, soon after the school opened in 1939.

Some of the Fairham Comprehensive School, Clifton, first-team soccer squad in 1973.

The Nottingham Evening Post

The *Nottinghamshire Guardian* was started by a consortium of 70 gentlemen in 1846 and was managed for them by Beverley Samuel Oliver. In 1848, Thomas Forman arrived in Nottingham to assist Oliver and in March the following year acquired the *Nottinghamshire Guardian* from the consortium. In 1852 a second paper, the *Midland Sporting Chronicle*, appeared from the Forman presses, followed by the *Midland Counties Observer* in 1857 and the *Daily Guardian* in 1861. In 1878, Thomas Forman published the first evening paper in the town, the *Nottingham Evening Post*. In 1953, his granddaughter Mrs D.K.Forman Hardy purchased the *Nottingham Journal, Evening News* and *Football News* from Westminster Press. These were eventually absorbed by the Forman group. For a short while, the names of these papers were coupled with the *Evening Post*. Nicholas J.Forman Hardy became chairman of T.Bailey Forman Ltd, publishers of the *Evening Post,* in August 1989. His father, Colonel T.E.Forman Hardy, great-grandson of the paper's founder Thomas Forman, had been chairman since October 1962. Colonel Forman Hardy died in September 1989. In December 1976 the *Evening Post* made newspaper history by publishing the first story in Great Britain ever to be 'set' by journalists, using a system of electronic editing developed by the *Evening Post* in conjunction with International Computers Ltd. There is now full screen make-up by journalists and methods are among the most advanced in the world. The *Evening Post* was Newspaper of the Year in 1991.

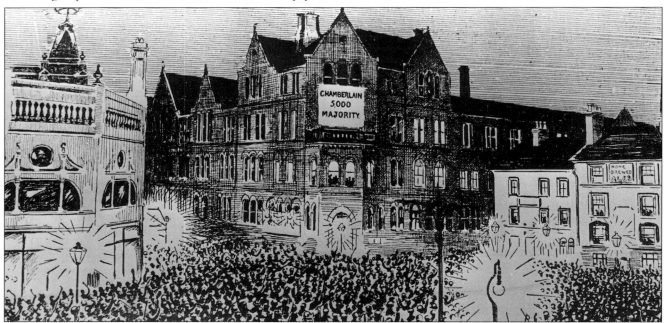

The crowd rejoices outside the Guardian office, in this drawing, as the banner proclaims 'Chamberlain 5,000 majority' in the 1906 General Election.

Making up pages on the stone. The compositors' room in the 1920s.

The sub-editors' room between the wars.

The Linotype room in 1929.

The new Computer Age editorial floor at the Evening Post.

Industrial Nottingham
– Lace

Nottinghamshire's Lace Market was never really a market open to the public, more a place for manufacturer, storage and visits by lace buyers. It started to develop, at the expense of spacious, elegant homes, after the introduction of Heathcote's lace machines of 1808, factories springing up with a vengeance by mid-century and beyond. By 1911, more than 22,000 people were employed in the lace trade but the bubble burst soon after the outbreak of World War One in 1914 and many companies went to the wall, in an area where fortunes once were made. Only the enterprise of firms such as the Birkin Group, the oldest Leavers lace manufacturers in the world, who eventually took lace into the computer age, saved the industry in Nottingham as it shrank dramatically while the hosiery trade prospered. The Lace Market itself, with its fine Victorian commercial architecture, became one of the City's first conservation areas in 1969.

This lace exhibition panel made in 1880 depicts scenes from Hamlet. It was part of a display at a Federation of Lace and Embroidery dinner in Nottingham in 1962, at which this picture was taken.

In Nottingham Lace manufacture, Jacquard cards determine the pattern and here, in October 1955, a Mr A.Hyson operates a machine that laces the cards together.

Industrial Nottingham
– Pure Drugs and Pharmaceuticals

In 1877, Jesse Boot put his name over his mother's little shop in Goose Gate, Nottingham, where he had worked since he was 13, and opened for business with jugs and jars of herbal remedies, the cupboards crammed with proprietary goods. By 1977 when Boots the Chemists celebrated its centenary, 1,250 shops bore his name and two out of three women in Britain shopped at them. Not bad for the son of a farm labourer who died when Jesse was ten. The first Boots pharmacist was appointed in 1884 and the following year Jesse started a complete manufacturing division. In his mid-30s he married Florence Rowe, daughter of a Jersey stationer, and she encouraged him to branch out into fashion, beauty, books, stationery and gifts. She devoted herself to the welfare of staff and when she learned that some of the poorer girls arrived at work without having breakfast, she ordered hot cocoa to start the day at Boots. The company bought a 300-acre factory site and a soap factory was built in 1927-28. Jesse Boot, first Lord Trent, died in 1931, after being crippled with arthritis. Ironic since this great benefactor had relieved the pain and suffering of millions. The traditions of Jesse and Florence were well maintained by their son John, the second Lord Trent and second chairman of Boots. He brought the company back into British ownership by 1933. In 1920 his father had sold control to the United Drug Company of America. Boots became not only a major manufacturer but also one of Britain's leaders in the development of research-based pharmaceuticals. Boots department stores, far bigger than anything Jesse could have envisaged, sprung up in major towns.

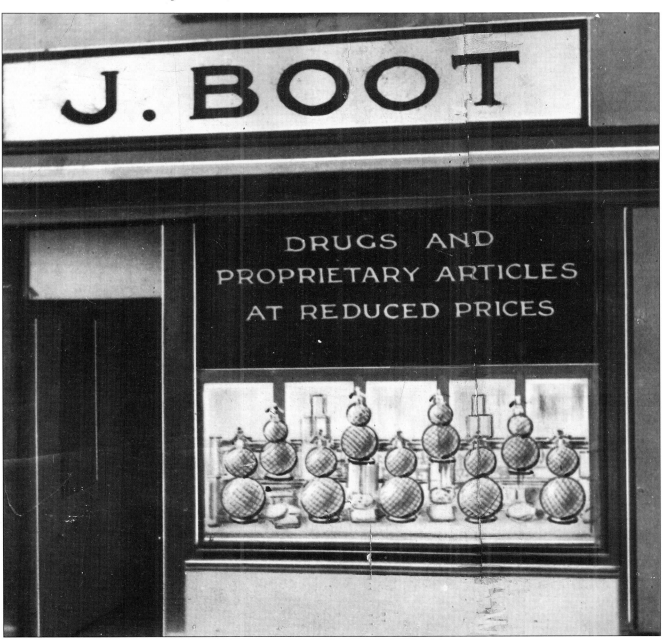

The first Boots shop, in Goose Gate, pictured in 1933.

The old Boots offices in Station Street.

A portrait of the first Lord Trent (Jesse Boot).

Left: The Boots tablet compressing department at Island Street between the wars. Right: Jesse Boot's first large-scale manufacturing base, the chemical and pharmaceutical works, Island Street, pictured in 1923.

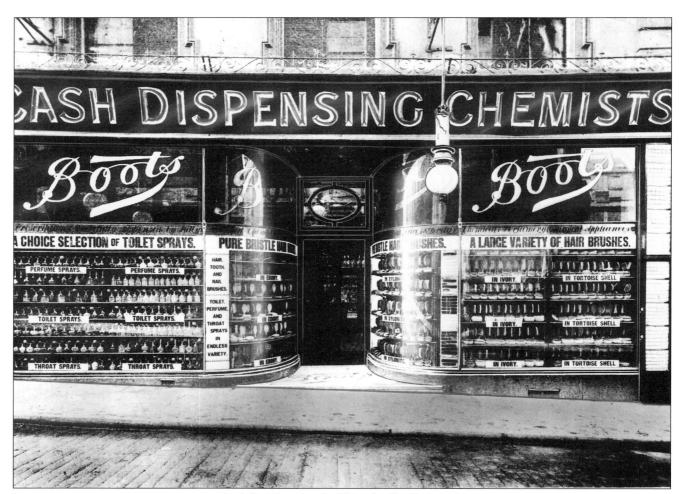

The Pelham Street branch of Boots the Chemists in 1896.

Industrial Nottingham
– Cigarettes and Tobacco

John Player, one of Nottingham's most famous adopted sons, came to the city from Saffron Walden. In 1877, he established a new industry which was to have far-reaching effects on the community. He set up shop on Beastmarket Hill as an agent for manures and seeds and started buying loose tobacco and selling it as a sideline. The sideline took over and 15 years after his arrival in Nottingham, he bought a tobacco factory in Broad Marsh and his marketing methods were so successful he was able to buy a site at Radford in the early 1880s, building three factory blocks, which became the nucleus of the 30 acres of factories and offices which were to grow on the site. The Castle tobacco factory was opened in 1884 but, sadly, he died a few months later at the age of 45 and the company was run by his friends until his sons, John

Dane Player and William Goodacre Player, were ready to take over in 1893. By 1898 the work-force had grown to 1,000. In 1901, faced with fierce competition from the mass production of American tobacco magnate James Buchanan Duke, John Player and Sons and 12 other leading British manufacturers formed the Imperial Tobacco Company. William and John Player, both great public benefactors, remained on the Imperial board until their retirement in 1926. There was considerable building expansion at Radford up to the outbreak of World War One with, by then, 2,500 employees, a figure which had grown to 7,500 by 1939. The biggest addition to John Player's operations came in 1972 with the opening of the Horizon factory on a 45-acre site at Lenton. It won three major architectural awards.

The original John Player shop in Nottingham.

A packet of Player's Navy Cut cigarettes and an advertisement for another famous brand, Weights.

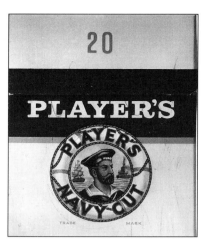

Bottom: John Player and Sons' showpiece Horizon factory which won the 1973 Financial Times Industrial Architecture Award after taking the Royal Institute of British Architects 1972 award for the East Midlands and the 1972 Civic Trust Award. The first cigarettes were produced in January 1972, some 29 months after construction began.

The John Player factory in Radford Boulevard.

Industrial Nottingham
– Bicycles

Raleigh cycles are almost as famous as Robin Hood, yet founder Frank Bowden survived a 'death sentence' to build up the greatest company of its kind in the world. Bowden, later Sir Frank, was only 28 when he returned from a trip to Hong Kong to be told he had only months to live. Instead he cycled his way to full fitness in six months, bought an interest in the tiny firm which made his bike in 1887, leading to the formation of the Raleigh Cycle Company, three years later. He bought a four-storey factory on Russell Street, then, in 1896, after spectacular growth, built what was at the time the largest cycle factory in the world on a seven and a half acre site on Faraday Road. By the time World War One broke out in 1914, Raleigh were producing 50,000 cycles a year. In 1960, Raleigh Industries merged with the TI (Tube Investments) Group, gaining control of the Phillips, Hercules, Norman and Sun brands to become the world's largest cycle producers. The company is still a major employer in the town.

The main entrance to Raleigh Industries' new Number Three factory on Triumph Road, which was opened by Field Marshall Lord Montgomery in September 1957.

Sir Harold Bowden, then the 72-year-old chairman of Raleigh Cycle Co, with his bride-to-be June Mackay Bowden in November 1952. She had changed her name by deed poll.

Sir Frank Bowden, father of Raleigh, watches over the production line.

A Raleigh workshop in about 1913.

Industrial Nottinghamshire
– Coal-mining

Coal dominated the west side of Nottinghamshire for centuries and pits were being worked at Wollaton, Strelley, Cossall and Selston in the thirteenth century. In 1832, coal owners met at the Sun Inn, Eastwood, to set up the Midland Counties Railway and the first train travelled from Nottingham to Derby in 1839. Sadly, closure after closure of pits around the county is likely to leave an industry with only five pits and 3,000 jobs. This compares with 31 pits and 40,000 workers as recently as 1981.

Tough conditions underground at Clifton Colliery in 1895.

Coal-cutting 1938 style. Machines took over but mining remains one of the toughest jobs there is.

A pit pony pulls a coal tub underground early this century.

Clifton Colliery pictured in 1936.

The message is clear in the 1984 strike.

Mr Hugh Gaitskell, Minister of Fuel (second left), with (left to right) Ald W.Bayliss, president of the Notts area NUM, Will Lather, national president of the NUM, and Sir Hubert Houldsworth, chairman of the East Midlands Division, NCB, at the Mineworkers Conference in the Technical College, Shakespeare Street, Nottingham, in November 1948.

A unique incident in the history of the TUC, a ballot in the Notts coalfield to discover whether a newly-formed company union had the support of the mineworkers, in 1928.

Jeff Orridge tosses a pancake while on picket duty at Wilford power station during the miners' strike in 1972.

Inset: Metropolitan Police officers link arms to force back NUM protesters at Thoresby Colliery in the 1984 miners' strike. Main picture: Miners' children join in a protest march to the Notts NUM headquarters, Berry Hill, Mansfield, during the 1984 strike.

Industrial Nottingham – Hosiery and Knitwear

William Lee, thought to have been born in about 1560 at Calverton, near Nottingham, was the founder of the industry. He invented a loom which spawned many generations of framework knitters. By the middle of the eighteenth century, Nottinghamshire had more than 3,000 frames, with 1,200 in Nottingham itself. James Hargreaves, inventor of the Spinning Jenny which produced several threads at once, moved to Nottingham in around 1767, partly to escape machine smashers in his native Lancashire and, even more significantly in the development of the cotton hosiery trade, Richard Arkwright, who later patented his roller-spinning machine, came to live in Nottingham in 1768. Nottingham lost out for a period when areas with water power ruled but the trade started to flourish again after the steam engine was adapted to drive machinery and by 1815 there were more than 30 mills in the county. It took the best part of a century to complete the transition from the cottage to the factory system of hosiery production and at times it was a very troubled road. The industry flourished in Nottingham and county for many decades, but in recent years, it has shrunk, not least because of cheap imports.

The Hargreaves Mill off Wollaton Street. It was erected in 1767 and used for ten years by James Hargreaves, inventor of the Spinning Jenny. It was the first cotton mill in the world but sadly it has been demolished.

Alfred Elsmore's oil painting The Origin of the Stocking Frame.

An old engraving of children sewing in a workhouse.

The remains of Johnson's mill on Forest Road West.

Hosiery machinery being set up at a Nottingham factory in 1949.

Yarn being spun at William Hollins' factory in July 1971.

It's a woman's world for Ian Clements, the only male machinist at Unwin Sportswear's Cranbrook Street factory in April 1976.

Work goes on at Meridian's factory in Haydn Road in September 1978.

The former Viyella factory in Castle Boulevard.

Nottingham Pubs

The Trip to Jerusalem, claimed to be the oldest inn in England. It was opened in 1189 and is said to have been popular with returning Crusaders. With cellars cut into Castle Rock, it is thought to have started as the Castle brewhouse.

The medieval Ye Olde Salutation Inn as it looked in 1950.

The Windmill Inn in Weekday Cross in 1970.

The Barley Mow on Weekday Cross.

The Fox and Grapes Inn, Sneinton, in 1937.

The Spread Eagle, Goldsmith Street in 1952 just before its demolition to make way for the extensions to the Nottingham and District Technical College.

Nottingham Churches

The mother church of Nottingham, St Mary's, pictured in January 1972. There was a church on the site in Norman times, probably even in Saxon times. Basically, it is now fifteenth-century perpendicular architecture at its best.

Some of the bells, the oldest of which dates back to 1595, awaiting removal from the churchyard at St Mary's Church in September 1934.

A memorial in St Mary's Church to officers, NCOs and men of the South Notts Hussars, who fell in World War One in Egypt, Gallipoli, Macedonia, Palestine and France. The picture was taken in January 1947, before a tablet and casket were added, containing a roll of honour in memory of members of the regiment who gave their lives in World War Two.

St Barnabas's Roman Catholic Cathedral, Derby Road, Nottingham, pictured in 1958.

A cloud of almond blossom in St Nicholas's Churchyard brings a touch of almost rural charm to the heart of the busy city in 1971. The church is also pictured.

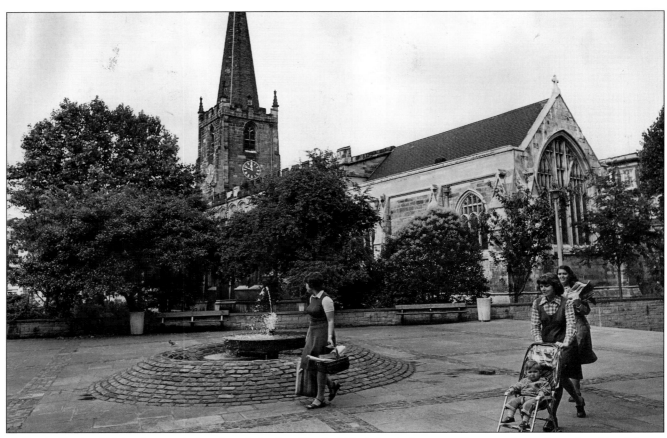

St Peter's Church, which is only a stone's throw from the hustle and bustle of Nottingham's city centre, offers a spot of peace for people making their way to Low Pavement and the surrounding shops.

The induction in 1948 of the Revd J.Loughlin by the Bishop of Southwell in the bombed-out St Christopher's Church, Colwick Road, Sneinton.

The partly demolished St Phillips Church in Pennyfoot Street, Nottingham, in October 1963.

A city resident goes to church . . .to collect firewood. St Ann's Church was being demolished as part of the area development scheme in 1971.

A sorry sight, in the cause of progress and the modernisation of Nottingham in July 1972. Emmanuel Church, Woodborough Road, in the final stages of its demolition. The Church on the Hill, as it was affectionately known, was being amalgamated with a new St Ann's Church in the heart of the redevelopment area. Emmanuel parish dates back to 1880. The last service at the church was in May of that year.

The notice board outside the Bridgeway Methodist Hall in Arkwright Street recalls that it opened its doors in 1864. This was taken in January 1965, prior to being replaced by another church 'more suited to modern needs'.

Housing and Other Developments

Arnold Road, looking east toward Daybrook in 1937, showing the first houses to be built on what is now the Bestwood Estate and (below) an aerial view of the estate.

The first tenants move in on Nottingham's giant Clifton Estate in 1951.

St Ann's in Nottingham starts to take on a new look in April 1970. Builders had torn down half the area and left what looked like a ghost town. This view is looking towards the Council House.

It is September 1970 and houses on either side of St Ann's Well Road take shape.

The St Ann's clearance goes on.

An aerial view of the St Ann's redevelopment in September 1970. The target was new homes for 17,000 people by 1976.

A demonstration in Nottingham Castle grounds of the first prefabs in Nottingham around 1950.

Prefabs go up in Nottingham in 1952.

Shopping with a difference in 1975 at the Balloon Wood flats, at the estate's food co-operative 'shop'.

Members of the Balloon Wood management committee and tenants stage a sit-in at the community centre to protest about conditions in April 1977.

The infamous Balloon Houses development which became known as Balloon Wood. Demolition started in December 1983.

The Victoria Centre site in 1968 as clearance work went on.

The end of Balloon Wood. A chain and ball smashes down part of the development.

Bolsover Square in the centre of Nottingham in November 1967, when it was little more than a wasteland and eyesore.

The square in 1969 after redevelopment following a council compulsory purchase order over which no objections were lodged. Residents were delighted with the tidying-up operation.

Work proceeds on the new Victoria Centre, with its high-rise flats to the right, in October 1971.

Member of Parliament Keith Speed opens the new Victoria Centre in March 1973.

A Nottingham Corporation bus becomes one of the first to negotiate the new Clifton Bridge in 1958.

The new Clifton Bridge, which opened in February 1958.

The scene at the new Clifton Bridge in August 1957, soon after the centre beam was put in place.

Princess Alexandra cuts the tape on the estate side of Clifton Bridge to officially open it in June 1958. At her side is the chairman of the general works and highways committee, Alderman E.Smith.

It Happened in Nottingham

Walking on the frozen river at Trent Bridge in 1895. Only Brian Clough has been able to do it since – without the ice!

A painting of the fire that destroyed Nottingham's trade exhibition of 1903. Nottingham got the blaze under control but not before Forest's football stand had caught alight.

The great fire at Nottingham's Albert Hall in April 1906. And the scene inside the hall after the blaze.

It's Coronation Day for George V on 22 June 1911, and a military procession marches along Derby Road, Nottingham.

An attentive audience for the Duke of Portland (out of picture) at the opening on the Nottingham Exposition in July 1938.

Firemen fight to save the old windmill in Sneinton in July 1947.

The fire, seen from Trent Bridge, which destroyed the wooden Main Stand at Nottingham Forest's City Ground on 24 August 1968.

A mounted policeman controls the crowd as the Main Stand at the City Ground goes up in flames.

How the Evening Post
reported the Coronation on
2 June 1953.

A carnival procession, many of the tableaux in which were presented by youth clubs, passes through Wheeler Gate as it toured the city on the eve of the Queen's Coronation.

Clayton Terrace, Hyson Green, all dressed up for the 1953 Coronation.

The 1947 Nottingham Floods

An Army duck takes people to and from their homes in the King's Meadow Road area in March 1947.

A torrent of flood water pouring from the LMS goods yard in Wilford Road during the floods.

Emergency meals in containers being loaded into an Army lorry in Kirkwhite Street for distribution in the flooded areas of Nottingham.

Residents look on in amazement as a car driver attempts to negotiate the floods in The Meadows.

A fire pump on its way to an urgent call in The Meadows.

An old, old story. Councillor J.Bagshaw talks to residents of Livingstone Terrace, Bunbury Street, The Meadows, after their homes were flooded in August 1967.

Canoe time in the streets of Bulwell during the floods.

Miners on their way to their shift at Clifton Colliery after severe flooding in April 1947.

A lorry forces its way along Lincoln Street, Old Basford, during the floods.

Residents find a way to get home in Jennison Street, Bulwell, during the 1947 floods.

Parts of Lincoln Street, Old Basford, well under water as the River Leen overflowed its banks, pouring water into houses and shops.

The swollen River Trent nearly tops the wall near Wilford Bridge while on the right, a car ploughs along the already flooded Colliery Road.

A resident in Brierley Street, The Meadows, fishes for coke which was floating past his house.

A dumper loaded with workers and shoppers in Wilford Road.

Goods are lowered to a customer from the bedroom window of a shop in New Bosworth Road, The Meadows.

Important Visitors to Nottingham

Cheering crowds greet the Prince of Wales during a visit to Boots in 1923.

Mahatma Gandhi visiting Nottingham in October 1931 to see his nephew, J. V. Joshi, a student at University College. And how the visit was reported at the time.

Workers at the Royal Ordnance Factory in King's Meadow Road, Nottingham, cheer King George VI during his visit in October 1939.

The Queen and the Duke of Edinburgh inspect the South Notts Hussars on The Forest Recreation Ground in 1955. They were in Nottingham for the Royal Show in Wollaton Park. With the Queen is the commanding officer, Lt-Col A.A.Warburton. With the Duke is Colonel (then Major) T.E.Forman Hardy, who commanded the saluting party.

Field Marshal Lord Montgomery on a visit to Nottinghamshire in October 1947.

Princess Margaret leaves the partly-built Church of St Francis during her tour of the Clifton Estate in May 1960.

Mrs Thatcher on a winning streak in Nottingham in December 1975. She won the champagne at tombola at the Sherwood Rooms.

The Prince and Princess of Wales wave to the crowd from the balcony of Nottingham's Council House, in 1985.

Excited onlookers get a close-up of the Princess of Wales in Nottingham in February 1989.

The Princess Royal delights the crowds during a visit to Nottingham in 1986.

Entertaining Nottingham

Elton John gives a stunning performance at the opening in November 1982 of the Royal Concert Hall and again at the same venue in December 1985.

Tom Jones arrives at Nottingham's Royal Centre in September 1983, on his first British tour for ten years.

Stan Laurel and Oliver Hardy on stage at the Nottingham Empire in January 1954 with a local act Bobbie Collins and Ginger.

Laurel and Hardy turn their hand to Christmas pudding-making at Nottingham's County Hotel in December 1953.

It was hard to keep a straight face when this pair got together. Two of Britain's best-loved comedy stars, Eric Sykes and Les Dawson, joined forces at Nottingham's Theatre Royal in October 1986 to star in Ray Cooney's farce Run For Your Life.

Harry Secombe signs a copy of his book Twice Brightly *outside a bookshop in Nottingham's Victoria Centre in November 1974, for Mrs Christine Harris of Radford.*

Harry Secombe with Elizabeth Larner (left) and Dorothy Wayne, who were appearing in Secombe Here *at the Theatre Royal in November 1962.*

Ken Dodd puts his tickling stick to good use during a visit to Nottingham in 1973.

It's Harry Secombe again entertaining a Nottingham crowd in July 1971.

An impromptu singalong for two of Nottingham's civic leaders, the Lord Mayor, Councillor Mrs Ivy Matthews (right) and the Lady Mayoress, Mrs Patricia Ann Matthews, with The Spinners in February 1976 during a visit to the Council House by the folk group, who were appearing at the city's Albert Hall. The Spinners are (left to right) Cliff Hall, Tony Davis (at the piano), Hughie Jones and Mick Groves.

Max Bygraves chats with Ham Manor professional Tommy Horton during the Parmeco Pro-Am tournament at Rushcliffe Golf Club in September 1971.

The great Arthur Askey shares a joke with some of the volunteer helpers at Nottingham's new Oxfam shop in Bridlesmith Gate which he opened in May 1970.

Tommy Steele has a bit of a knees-up with the Lord Mayor and Lady Mayoress of Nottingham, Councillor and Mrs Stan Rushton, to celebrate his 20 years in show business, in September 1976. He tried out the acoustics of the Theatre Royal ready for his anniversary show there the following month.

The Commodore
Banqueting Rooms,
Aspley, in 1969, after
large-scale alterations,
mainly to the
ballroom.

The cast of the comedy Once a
Catholic at the Theatre Royal,
Nottingham, don safety gear to
look around the shell of the new
Concert Hall, under construction
at the rear of the theatre in July
1981, soon after the first roof
truss was fitted.

Issy Bonn (right) with Bill Maynard next to him, and the King Brothers, who were all appearing at the Empire Theatre, Nottingham, in January 1958.

The line-up at the Nottingham Empire in July 1898.

*The Hippodrome Theatre in Nottingham
later became the Gaumont, as the 1971
picture (right) shows.*

The new Palace Theatre music-hall, as seen from Trent Bridge in 1927.

Nottingham author Alan Sillitoe, whose book Saturday Night and Sunday Morning *was based in the city and became a smash-hit film, chats to Mrs Pat O'Connell, leader of anti-Polaris submarine marchers, during a protest meeting in Old Market Square in April 1961.*

Gracie Fields tells an audience of 2,000 at Nottingham's Albert Hall in 1952, "I'm in Love with a Wonderful Guy". She was a regular visitor to Nottingham after appearing as a member of juvenile troops at the Empire, Hippodrome and Theatre Royal.

Nottingham at Leisure

Twisting the time away. A group of Nottingham girls get in the groove to a portable record-player on the steps of Victoria Embankment, Nottingham, in April 1962.

Nottingham model girls collecting for Cancer Relief at the Nottingham Festival race meeting at Colwick Park in July 1970.

A group of Nottingham Festival hostesses take a breather in Old Market Square in July 1970, before setting out to attend the day's events.

Although the leaves are beginning to fall, the weather is still warm enough, in October 1960, for visitors to enjoy an airing in the grounds of Nottingham Castle.

The scene at the Roundhouse Theatre, Wollaton Park, in July 1970, when Nottingham Playhouse company presented a play for children.

A stroll in Nottingham Castle grounds for these two pretty girls in June 1960.

Tobogganing in full swing on the slopes of The Forest in January 1952.

Baseball as played by US forces on American Independence Day (4 July) draws a big crowd at The Forest, Nottingham. The year the picture was taken is not known.

A procession of carnival bands marching through Aspley in August 1936.

Left: All fall down . . .the collapse of a light-hearted tug-o'-war team which took part in games at a play leadership scheme at Sycamore Recreation Ground, Nottingham, in July 1968. Right: A game of football on Robin Hood's Chase in August 1958.

Sporting Nottingham

A handshake for Tommy Lawton (left) from Notts County manager Arthur Stollery after Lawton's record signing from Chelsea in November 1947.
Inset: Another copybook bullet header from Tommy Lawton, for Notts County against Queen's Park Rangers.

Nottingham welcomes home its FA Cup winners, Nottingham Forest, in 1959. The players acknowledge the crowds from a coach at Canning Circus and salute them in Old Market Square.

Nottingham Forest outside-right Roy Dwight, who scored a goal and then broke his leg in the 1959 Cup Final, gets a kiss of congratulation and commiseration from his wife Connie at Wembley General Hospital. Dwight, incidentally, is an uncle of pop star Elton John. .

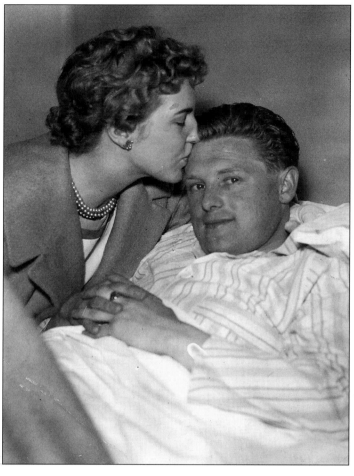

The masterminds behind Nottingham Forest's history-making successes, Peter Taylor (left) and Brian Clough, in April 1978.

"We've done it again" – Nottingham Forest and England goalkeeper Peter Shilton kisses the European Cup after Forest's 1-0 win in the Final against SV Hamburg in 1980.

Nottingham Forest captain John McGovern and defender Larry Lloyd parade the European Cup after Forest had beaten Malmö 1-0 in the 1979 Final. Present manager Frank Clarke (centre) follows them down the steps with Garry Birtles behind Lloyd and Kenny Burns (right).

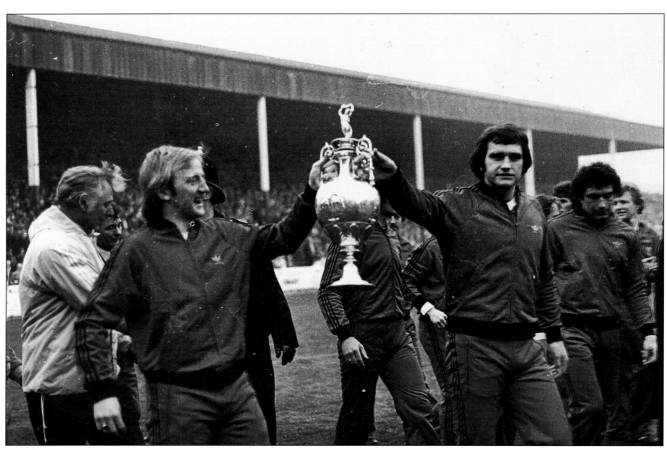

"We are the champions" – Nottingham Forest defenders Kenny Burns (left) and Larry Lloyd, head the parade at the City Ground after Forest won the old First Division title in 1978. Peter Taylor and (behind him) Brian Clough are on the left and goalkeeper Peter Shilton on the right.

The end of an era as Notts County's Meadow Lane stand is demolished in July 1978. It was thought to have been the oldest in active use in England. Formerly owned by Nottinghamshire County Cricket Club, the 1,400-seat structure was floated across the River Trent in 1910.

Notts County manager Jimmy Sirrel
urges his team on in a match in April
1973. Sirrel coaxed Notts through all
four divisions of the Football League
after joining them in 1969. He had a
two-season spell with Sheffield
United in the mid-1970s, then
returned to push County into the
First Division by 1981. He
concentrated on youth development
when Larry Lloyd was appointed
manager but took over the reigns
again at the age of 63 in August
1985, as first Lloyd and then his
successor Richie Barker were
dismissed. Sirrel was later chief scout
at Derby County.

Nottinghamshire County Cricket Club players leaving the pavilion at Trent Bridge during a match against the Australians in 1911. Notts won by six wickets.

Two studies of the
legendary Harold
Larwood, as a bowler in
his prime around 1933,
and as a batsman in
April 1935.

Overseas cricketing maestros, South African Clive Rice (left) and New Zealander Richard Hadlee celebrate a magnificent double, the Britannic Assurance Championship and the NatWest Bank Trophy in September 1987.

Chick Zamick, Nottingham Panthers' new coach (standing, right), talks tactics with players at the start of the 1955-56 season. They are, (left to right) Al Watson, Doug Wilson, Dave Ritchie, Lorne Smith, Bill Ringer and Les Strongman. Zamick had an illustrious playing career with Panthers.

British welterweight champion Wally Swift gets a helping hand, in November 1960, from his nine-year-old brother Neil Swift as he prepares to defend his title against Brian Curvis at Nottingham Ice Rink. Swift, then a cycle assembler, won the British title at both welter and middleweight.

Play in progress in the opening round of the Victory Shield bowls competition on Nottingham's Sycamore Road green in July 1939.

Former world heavyweight champion Joe Louis, right, at the Albany Hotel, Nottingham, in January 1973. He was special guest at a boxing show at the Ice Rink. With him is promoter Mickey Duff.

Nottingham's own Torvill and Dean, the greatest duo in the history of ice dancing, make a triumphant return to the city in September 1985 in their spectacular in a giant marquee on The Forest. Jayne and Christopher won British, European Olympic and World titles before turning professional. They made a brief return to the British, European and Olympic stage in 1994 after rule changes allowed them to compete again but, through disappointment and controversy during the Olympic games, they returned again to the professional circuit and didn't compete in the World Championships.

Christopher Dean on the beat in the centre of Nottingham in 1980.

Subscribers

J Abraham
Maureen Aitken
Mr H Aldridge
J Frobisher Alltoft
John Anderson
Mr Robert Anderson
John Andrews
Lilian Anthony
Allison Armstrong
Mrs Roma Ashworth
Ernest J Astill
Robert & Anne Atkins
Andrew Auckland
Rolfe Ayres
Terence E Balchin
Lionel Vincent Ball
Alan Bamford
Mrs Barbara
Gerald P Barnes
John D Barrowcliffe
Mr Frank Bell (USA)
George A S Bell
June Bennett
Mrs Anne Benson
Patricia Bestwick
Susan I Bevan
Mrs Joan E Bexon
A R Bickerton
Ian Paul Biddulph
Jean Ann Biddulph
B Bignall
Mr D S Bilbie
Mr H F Billings
A T Billson
Hannah Birch
Mr J A Birch
T W Birch
G H Bird
Barry Birkhead

Paul A Bloomer
Anthony Booth
Mr John G Booth
Max Booth
A Booton
Mr & Mrs P G Boultby
Sheryl June Bowles
A S Bowley
Claire Bradley
Margaret R Bradley
Victor Brett
Paul Brewster
Mrs Jean A Brinsley
John Brock
Barbara Brooke
Mr Edgar Brooke
Mrs Lily Brooks
P J Brooksbank
Janet Brown
Mrs Kathleen E Brownlow
H S Burchell
Frederick Burton
W R E Burton
Lucy M Butt
Miss E Callow
Patricia Calvert
Brian Camm
D G Camm
Mr Patrick Campbell
Mrs A Campion
Ronald Carrier
Mrs I Carrington
R M Carter
S B Cash
Alec Casterton
Helen Westray Cawthan
Mr Ted Chamberlain
Timothy Chamberlin
Mr Gerald Chambers

Mrs S A Chambers

Geoffrey Chapman

Dr M J Chappell

Harland Chester

Mrs I M Ciupruk

Mrs C R Clark

Mrs M Clark

Tom & Peg Clark

Mr Dennis Clarke

Mr Tony Clarke

Mr Peter Clegg

Mrs C M Colton

Edith Anne Connelly

Eric Cook

Peter F Cooke

Mr & Mrs Cowdell

William L Cramp

Gladys Crosland

Reg Croxford

J A Dale

M W Davies

Marion A Davis

Mr E Day

Sarah Daykin

Jill & Christopher Dean

John Deaton

Cyril Denning

A J & S Dexter

John Evatt Dexter

Marylyn Dickens

Dorothy May Disney

John Edward Dixon

Terry G B Donlan

Mrs A Doody

M A L Draycott

Elizabeth Dudson

Leonard Dunstan

B E Eaton

Jonathan M Eaton

Mrs J M Edwards

Mr J Edwards

M A Edwards

Michael Edwards

P G Edwards

Vera Irene Edwards

Mr & Mrs Harry C Elliott

Mr F Emerson

Mr & Mrs R N Epton

Charles Ewart

Margaret Ann Fearn

Phyllis Felose-Summers

Edwin John Felton

Mr Stuart Fenton & Mrs Pauline
     Fenton

Mrs K I Ferguson

Anthony Fisher

Mr T W Fletcher

Margaret Ann Ford

Graham Fowler

Mrs H Fowler

C M Foxon

Mrs Pauline Francis

Leonard Franks

Jean Frayne

Joan Fritchley

Mrs Grace Fyles

Mrs D Gamble

Mrs D Gamble

Mr R G Garner

Mr Harold Francis Gascoyne

Joan & Jack Gibson

Stephen Giles

Peter Gill

Richard J Gill

A L Glover

Jon & Joanne Glover

Mary Godward

Peter Derek Gough

Peter Derek Gough

Jonathan Gregory

Mr Frank Grice

Mr R O Griffiths

Mrs Jacqueline Haddon

Brenda M Hadley

Anthony Gordon Hales

Mr Frank Hallam

Isabel Handbury

G M Hardman

Edward G & Betty J Hardy

Charles Harriman

Everett W Harrison

G E Hart

Mr G Hatwood

Mr J H Hawkins

Martin Robert Hawley

Mr H J Hayes

Derek Hazard

George Henshaw

Kay Hill

Roger Hill

Alan Hind

Mr E F L Hodges

Fred & Ida Hodgkinson

John Holland

W E Hollingsworth

Peter Holmes

James Thomas Hopewell

John Hopewell

Ann & Neville Hoskins

I D Houghton

Pete Howarth

Simon John Hoyle

Mr & Mrs D I Hudson

Mr & Mrs D I Hudson

Kevin & Pauline Hull

R L Hulsman

D R Hustwayte

Peter Hutchinson

Doreen P Huttyn

Vera Iremonger

David Jackson

Don Jackson

Donald Jackson

Doreen M Jackson

Mrs Jean Jackson

Mavis Jackson

Glennys Johnson

Stephanie Johnstone

Mrs Maureen Jones

T & M E Jones

T & M E Jones

Gerald G Justice

Mr K Kelleher

Sidney Whitehall Kelly

Mrs M Kelvey

Mrs M Kelvey

Roy Douglas Kilner

Mrs Barbara E King

Richard Neil Kirk

Audrey & Richard Lambert

Mr S Land

Malcolm Lane

Jean Langham

P W Langridge

Mr D B Lawrence

E J Lawrence

D P Lawson

Roy Leadbeater

Stanley Leatherland

Kenneth Leech

Neil Lewin

Colin M Lightfoot

Mrs P Lill

John William Lock

Mrs M L Long

Bryan Lonsdale

Harold Loseby

Arthur Lovatt

Mr K R Luxon

Marjorie McCann

Ian James McClair

Eric Macdonald

Kathleen Mace

M McInerney

John & Tony Mackness

Mr Malcolm Macleod

Duke Manners

Sheila Manners

Mrs Mary Mannington (formerly
      Hughes)

Mr G W Mantle

Mr & Mrs S G Marks

Mr John Marlow

Mrs Greta Maroni

Paul Marshall

L F Martin

Reginald Martin

T J Martin

Michael Mathers

Mr & Mrs C Matthewson

Stuart Meakin

Mr H E Mettham

Mr & Mrs E Middleton

Mrs G Millband

Norman Miller

Ronald James Miller

Geoffrey Mills

Mr M A Minns

Mrs E M Moore

Kenneth Morley

Steven Thomas Morley

Mrs A Morris

Mrs Dorothy Morris

Mrs L Morris

Robin M Morris

Mr Eric Morrison

Brenda Morroz, Canada

William George Munks

Kath Munton

Mrs Olive Murden

Mrs Murray

Robert Nattrass

J Naylor

Mr L Naylor

Avril Nelson

Paul Robert Nesbitt

Brian David Newbert

Mr E W Nicholson

Harry Norris

John James Norwebb

Mrs D O'Conner

William O'Dell

George David Oliver

A B & F M O'Malley

Mrs B O'Sullivan

Robert Otter

Deryk J Page

G B Page

Mrs D Paine

William J Parker

Mr F Parr

Colin John Pearce

Robert Peatman

Mr & Mrs A Peberday

Frank Pepper

Margaret Rose Perry

Miss M J Phillips

Mr Walter & Sheila Pike

Mrs Glenis Ping

Richard Pinkett

Mr J Plumb

Roy Plumb

Andrew Porter

Mr & Mrs Jack Poyner

Kathleen M Price

Mrs J H Prichard

S T Prichett

Mrs K M Prickard

David Alan Priestley

Gillian M Pygott

Miriam Quail
Mrs W D Rawson
Mr K J Reddington
Mrs Ann Reeve
Ivy Reeves
D Reynolds
Robert Bruce Rice
R E Richardson
Mr Ronald Richmond
D D Ridgway
F Rigley
Jessie Robinson
Peter Robinson
Mr & Mrs E Roebuck
Paul Rolfe
Mr D W Rook
M W Rossiter
G G Rothwell
Carl R Roulstone
Mr R Routhan
S Rowlson
P W Sawyer
Joseph Scarborough
L L Searson
William Sedgwick
Mr W B Sefton
Catherine Seymour
Kenneth G Sharpe
M A Shaw
E Shepperson
Anne Shipman
Margaret & David Sibley
Mr W E J Sims
Elizabeth Mary Singer
Freda Sketchley
George H Sleaford
Raymond Sleaford
Mr N G Smethurst
Miss C Smith
D Smith

D Smith
Gladys Smith
J H Smith
M Snellgrove
Joan Spencer
Walter Spencer
C L Spridgeon
Mrs M Squires
Mrs Doris Stacey
Mrs Valerie Stanley
P R Stapleton
Mr A Stephens
George Stevens
Samuel Henry Stevens
Joyce Stevens (née Payne)
Christine Stevenson
Sue & Alan Stimson
L K Stockdale
C G Stones
Mr Wilfred Storer
D T Strickland
Mr T Stubbs
C Stuchfield
B J Swann
B J Swann
Harry Swann
Ian Swift
Mr Kenneth B Swinson
E E Tame (née Watthey)
K W Tantum
David J Taverner
Roy Leslie Taylor
Trevor Peter Temperton
Mrs Jean Terry
A R Tew
Mr A C Thomas
June Thompson
Stewart Thornhill
G A Thornton
P J Tilley

Reginald Tomlinson
W A Towers
M G Towlson
Mr G & Mrs P Tunnicliffe
David G Tutin
C A Tyler
S H & E M Undy
Mr A A Ungless
Charles Joseph Uttley
Edmund Frederick Varney
Edmund Frederick Varney
Colin H Vaughan
Michael Vaughan
Mr M Vickers
Eric Vincent
Albert Edward Walker
George Moorby Walker
Robert Barrie Wall
N & K Wallis
Charlie Walmsley
Mr S I Walters
Mrs Doris M Waltham
Dorothy Ward
James Ward
Leonard Henry Warsop
Terence Weatherbed
Sheila Welch
Jonathan Wells
Sydney O Westmoreland
David Wharton
David Wharton
Mr E P White
Edward White
Raymond White
John R Whitfield
Michael J Whiting
O R Whiting
W Whitmore
Mr L Whittaker
Ellen Whittlesey

Mrs F M Wicks
Mr Graham Wilkins
J Williams
Mrs Shirley Williams
Joan Willis
B Willis
Brian Wilson
Ramon Winfield
Keith Winter
David A Wiseman
Georgine Wood
Thomas Wood
J G Woodward
Maureen Woodward
Pauline A Woodward
Charles Richard Woolsey
Mrs Mary Wray
Jack Wright
Mrs Wyer
Mr & Mrs A N Yeo
Leonard V Young
Mr W Young
Ms M Yuill